WELLS, ALTARS, AND OFFERINGS

Digging Deeper, Building Better, Giving More

John Stanko

Wells, Altars, and Offerings
by John W. Stanko
Copyright ©2023 John W. Stanko

ISBN 978-1-63360-251-9

For Worldwide Distribution
Printed in the U.S.A.

Urban Press
P.O. Box 8881
Pittsburgh, PA 15221-0881
412.646.2780
www.urbanpress.us

Table of Contents

Introduction

Every year, I send a book or two to those on my mailing list who have supported and contributed to my ministry. I was seeking the Lord to determine what I could send in 2023, and I've learned to pay attention to what I talk about on my broadcasts or in coaching and counseling sessions during such times of seeking. As has happened so often, that awareness was indeed the key to writing and compiling this book.

First, I met with one of the authors from my publishing company, Urban Press, and we got to talking about the story of Hagar in Genesis 19. I use that story as an example of God opening someone's eyes to the realities around them that were there all along, but their thinking or assumptions prevented them from seeing clearly.

Then, I was working on editing a message that I had preached on Jesus' encounter with the woman at the well in John 4. When I did, the lights came on for me. In Genesis 19, God showed Hagar a well that was right in front of her. Where did Jesus meet with the woman in John 4? He met her in Samaria—at a well when she came to fetch water.

There's a popular emoji that shows the top of someone's head "blowing up" from a mind-altering experience and it applies to when I saw the similarity between the two stories. Since these two encounters happened in the same general vicinity, my question was, *Could this well have been the same well in both stories?* While the Bible doesn't support that thought one way or the other, the fact remains that God used a well in both instances to minister to those two abused and forlorn women.

That insight caused me to reflect on other times that a water well was featured prominently in a Bible story since the characters all lived in the arid area of Palestine and its environs, I didn't have to search hard or think long on that matter. Along the way of my studies, I noticed one other thing. When Abraham and others ventured into an area, they not only dug a well to take care of their water needs, they also erected an altar to tend to their spiritual needs. And of course, altars were built as a place to give offerings to the Lord.

Now I had a possible theme for this book—wells, altars, and offerings—but didn't really have time to write it—or so I thought. It was then that

I began to go through the things I had already written over the years for my blog, in the *Monday Memo*, and for my weekly online Bible study. When I dug through my archives, I found I had a few dozen entries on all three topics. All I had to do was copy, paste, edit, and voila! You have what you are holding in your hand and reading: *Wells, Altars, and Offerings.*

My objective for this project is to help you "dig deeper, build higher, and give more." A well isn't a well until water is found, so the digger has to keep going until they reach their goal. They aren't sure how far it will be until they reach their objective. The same is true for you. When you set a significant goal, you neither know how long it will take to complete nor everything you will have to go through to find your water. I hope that the well entries will inspire you to stay the course to keep working and digging.

Then when you build your altar, I want you to build it big and strong. What is your altar? It's your visible expression of worship. I'm not referring to the songs you sing in church or private devotions, but your life purpose and creativity God has assigned you. There's no more significant act of worship than to express who God made you to be, for you honor Him by accepting your uniqueness and showcasing it for all to see. In fact, Paul wrote in Romans 12:1-2,

> Therefore, I urge you, brothers and sisters, in view of God's mercy, to offer your bodies as a living sacrifice, holy and pleasing to God—this is your true and proper worship. Do not conform to the pattern of this world, but be transformed by the renewing of your mind. *Then you will be able to test and approve what God's will is—his good, pleasing and perfect will* (emphasis added).

The ultimate sacrifice you can make is to know and do God's will. A sacrifice in this context isn't doing something for God that you were initially reluctant to do and then magnanimously decided to do. Rather it's acknowledging that you belong to God for Him to use as He sees fit, so you give to God what already belongs to Him—a sacrifice of obedience. Your purpose, the will of God for your life, is the ultimate expression of worship, for it accepts God's ownership of and Lordship over your life—which leads to the third theme of this book.

Every altar was erected to offer sacrifices, where some of God's creatures' lives were taken in the interests of worshiping Him. That's why I decided to include a few entries that focus on the Old Testament sacrifices, which I have studied for many years because they provide such a poignant picture of Christ and His relationship to the Father and His people. They are included to inspire you to give more, to devote yourself more completely to finding and fulfilling your purpose.

For me, part of my God-given life assignment is writing and publishing, and I have produced dozens of my own books and even more for others through Urban Press. Publishing is my altar and I am working on making it a significant and substantial one. One of the sacrifices of the worship on my altar (God's will) is represented in this book and I hope the entries will inspire you to play big and not hold back for fear that you're getting ahead of the Lord by going too far or giving too much.

How can you get ahead of the Lord when He is able to do "exceeding abundantly beyond all you could ask or think"? (Ephesians 3:20). His ability to do "the beyond all you can ask or think" is limited by the rest of that verse, which says, "according to his power that is at work within us." If there's no power working in you, then there's no "exceeding abundantly" on God's part. You have to do your part by nurturing and drawing on His power, and then He does His part. I want to increase your power which will in turn release His power in and through your life's work.

What To Expect?

The format of this book follows the one used in most of my other projects. My objective isn't just to teach you but to help you apply what you've been taught as quickly as possible, as Jesus advised us to do: "Now that you know these things, you will be blessed if you do them" (John 13:17). Toward that end, I include questions in every chapter to give you some ideas of what to do with what you have just read. Usually, the questions are in bold letters so they "jump out" at you, for I consider them the most important part of each chapter.

The entries are in random order so there's no need to read from start to finish unless that's the way you normally read. If you would rather treat this book like a box of chocolates and pick around to find and read what strikes your fancy, that's fine too. And as you would expect if you are familiar with my work, you'll find the topics of creativity and purpose well represented in the entries I chose.

That's because I "borrowed" some of the

entries from my Old Testament series, *The Purpose Study Bible*, along with my New Testament series, *Live the Word*, and *The Monday Memo*. Each of those series helps readers discover what I call the five Goldmine Principles of purpose, creativity, goal setting, time management, and faith. If you're going to dig deeper and build higher, you will need to rely on those five Principles to do so. Some of the entries are short, while others are a bit longer. Some are in the format of a commentary with passage and narrative, others are more in essay format.

I guess I should alert you that two entries aren't about a well, altar, or offering at all, but rather focus on a tower. You probably know which tower I am referring to, and I include it because I see the Tower of Babel as an altar gone awry. It became a monument to mankind's desire to do their own thing as opposed to God's. It shows that we will all build and dig something and therefore it's incumbent upon us that we dig, build, and offer for God's glory and not our own.

I think that covers everything you need to know, so now it's time to start reading *Wells, Altars, and Offerings: Digging Deeper, Building Better, Giving More*. May God direct and inspire you in the coming pages to erect and drill, to go higher and deeper in Him, and to produce something that will not only sustain you but also be a source of blessing for others. Happy digging and building!

John W. Stanko
Pittsburgh, PA USA
November 2023

1
Build Some Altars

As we study the earlier parts of Abram's life, we see that he used his creativity to build an altar wherever he settled:

- Abram traveled through the land as far as the site of the great tree of Moreh at Shechem. At that time the Canaanites were in the land. The Lord appeared to Abram and said, "To your offspring I will give this land." So he built an altar there to the Lord, who had appeared to him (Genesis 12:6-7).

- From there he went on toward the hills east of Bethel and pitched his tent, with Bethel on the west and Ai on the east. There he built an altar to the Lord and called on the name of the Lord (Genesis 12:8).

- From the Negev he went from place

to place until he came to Bethel, to the place between Bethel and Ai where his tent had been earlier and where he had first built an altar. There Abram called on the name of the Lord (Genesis 13:3-4).

- So Abram went to live near the great trees of Mamre at Hebron, where he pitched his tents. There he built an altar to the Lord (Genesis 13:18).

Abram was pursuing the purpose God had assigned him, but the way was hard and fraught with uncertainty and danger. Even his nephew and he experienced conflict in their relationship, which caused them to part ways—with Lot taking what appeared to be the best of the land when Abram allowed him to choose. At a time when it appeared Abram had experienced great loss, the Lord appeared to him and renewed His promises:

The Lord said to Abram after Lot had parted from him, "Look around from where you are, to the north and south, to the east and west. All the land that you see I will give to you and your offspring forever. I will make your offspring like the dust of the earth, so that if anyone could count the dust, then your offspring could be counted. Go, walk through the length and breadth of the land, for I am giving it to you" (Genesis 13:14-17).

What was Abram's response after Lot left and Lord spoke to him? He built an altar as described in Genesis 13:18, using his hands and creativity to worship the Lord and recommit his way to the God who was leading him. Your purpose and creativity are from the Lord and will only be fully expressed and realized in the context of worshiping Him. You're neither alone nor are you strong or smart enough to fulfill God's purpose in your own understanding and strength.

Are you building your own kingdom or building altars of worship and sacrifice with your gifts, time, and talents? Is it time for you to build an altar and worship the Lord right where you are with what you have? Are you mindful of God's presence and leading in the midst of your success and failure as you carry out His assignment for you?

Remember that worship, and not success as your culture defines it, is the goal of your life's efforts.

2
The Altar Of
Personal Sacrifice

In the previous entry, we looked at the four altars Abram built in response to the Lord's promises and presence in Abram's journey from the land of Ur to the land God had shown him was to be his. In this chapter, we look at another altar Abraham built, this one his fifth and most important:

> Abraham took the wood for the burnt offering and placed it on his son Isaac, and he himself carried the fire and the knife. As the two of them went on together, Isaac spoke up and said to his father Abraham, "Father?" "Yes, my son?" Abraham replied. "The fire and wood are here," Isaac said, "but where is the lamb for the burnt offering?" Abraham answered, "God himself will provide the lamb for the burnt offering, my son."

And the two of them went on together. When they reached the place God had told him about, Abraham built an altar there and arranged the wood on it. He bound his son Isaac and laid him on the altar, on top of the wood. Then he reached out his hand and took the knife to slay his son (Genesis 22:6-10).

This altar had to be big enough so Abraham could lay Isaac on it, probably made of stone with the wood for the fire under it and in the center created by a stone border. The fire under this altar had to be sufficient to convert Isaac to a burnt offering so it's safe to assume this wasn't a small altar as it has been depicted in some artistic renditions.

Abraham had to build all five altars in Genesis with his own hands, including this one, and God was also directing him to sacrifice his only son with those same hands. The lesson is that what you do through your purpose and with your creativity is ultimately for Him, no matter how many people you touch or serve. You must always keep your results in proper perspective and be willing to change course or surrender what you have been doing to His direction and will. Paul explained this dynamic in Jesus' life in his letter to the Philippians:

In your relationships with one another, have the same mindset as Christ Jesus: Who, being in very nature God, did not consider equality with God something to be used to his own advantage; rather, he made himself nothing by taking the very nature of a servant, being made in human likeness. And being found in appearance as a man, he humbled himself by becoming obedient to death—even death on a cross! (Philippians 2:5-8).

Are you placing all that you have and what is most important to you on the altar of worship in the service of others? Are you not only willing for God to take what you offer, but are you also building the altar—regularly and consciously *willing* to stop doing what it is that has become so meaningful to you as well as a source of godly fruit? Can you worship the Lord in times of loss or seasons of meager results as well as times of fulfilled promise and purpose plenty?

Abraham didn't go to sacrifice Isaac as a means to get God to change His mind. He wasn't thinking, "Oh, if I go through with this, maybe I can still save my son." In his mind, his son was dead and God was going to do something miraculous because of the promise He had given about Isaac's future. Abraham had totally and completely given his son to the Lord and God wants you to do the same thing, for only then can God's promise to you become all that it can be.

3
What's In A Name?

In Genesis 2, we see the account of Adam naming the animals which, when you think of it, was an example of his God-given creativity. God directed Adam's work but Adam was free to name the animals whatever he chose. We see another example of this kind of creativity as we finish up our study of Abraham's sacrifice of Isaac in Genesis 22:

> Abraham looked up and there in a thicket he saw a ram caught by its horns. He went over and took the ram and sacrificed it as a burnt offering instead of his son. So Abraham called that place The Lord Will Provide. And to this day it is said, "On the mountain of the Lord it will be provided" (Genesis 22:13-14).

When Abraham found the ram, he saw the day of the Lord as Jesus described in John 8:56-59:

> "Your father Abraham rejoiced at the

thought of seeing my day; he saw it and was glad."

"You are not yet fifty years old," they said to him, "and you have seen Abraham!"

"Very truly I tell you," Jesus answered, "before Abraham was born, I am!" At this, they picked up stones to stone him, but Jesus hid himself, slipping away from the temple grounds.

At that moment, Abraham was standing on Mt. Moriah, the eventual location of the Temple in Jerusalem where the story in John 8 played out, and close to where the ultimate sacrifice would take place through the death of Christ. When Abraham sacrificed the ram, he understood that God had sent a substitutionary sacrifice for Isaac to die in his son's place, just like God would send His Son as the Lamb of God to be slain for the forgiveness of our sins. Then Abraham did something that Adam had also done: he used his creativity to define the moment.

Abraham assigned a name to God that is still used by the people of God. Abraham looked at the ram, sacrificed it, considered what had taken place, summarized in his mind what had happened, and called the place *Jehovah-Jireh: the*

Lord Will Provide. Abraham saw that God would provide a sacrifice for Himself on His holy mountain and gave that place and God a new name.

We don't see that God directed Abraham to name the place. God didn't say to him, "Assign me a name now, according to what you have just seen." We certainly don't see that God was offended by what Abraham did. Abraham used his God-given ability to assess, evaluate, and create, and in a few words summarized what could have taken many more words to adequately communicate— *The Lord Will Provide.*

God has given you the same capacity as Abraham had. **Where can you use your creativity to assess and create? Is it the name of your company? The title for your book? The trend in your field of work? An invention? A movement? A child? A nickname that will lovingly connect someone with their heritage or talent? Your sense of humor? Your ability to write, paint, sculpt, or rhyme?**

Who knows, maybe as you express your creativity, the identifying title you give it could become a lasting memorial to your creativity and God's work in your life just like it did for Abraham. Then you can answer the question, "What's in a name?" by honestly saying, "the creativity that

God gave me is in that name"—and God will be honored to be identified with your creativity, just as He was with Abraham's.

4

Go Where
You're Celebrated

Isaac wasn't the most dynamic man highlighted in the Bible, but God still used him to continue Abraham's legacy. In Genesis we read,

> Isaac's servants dug in the valley and discovered a well of fresh water there. But the herders of Gerar quarreled with those of Isaac and said, "The water is ours!" So he named the well Esek [dispute], because they disputed with him. Then they dug another well, but they quarreled over that one also; so he named it Sitnah [opposition]. He moved on from there and dug another well, and no one quarreled over it. He named it Rehoboth [room], saying, "Now the Lord has given us room and we will flourish in the land" (Genesis 26:19-22, meaning of words in brackets added by author].

Before he dug those three wells, Isaac had been asked to leave his previously-occupied territory because he was too powerful and the locals feared his presence. So he left, only to encounter the opposition and dispute over the first two wells that he dug to water his abundant flocks. Isaac kept moving on until he came to another place, dug a well, and found no opposition. He named that place Rehoboth because God had finally made a place or room for him.

The same can happen when you pursue your purpose. You can be a threat to others so you have to move on. Then you have some other successes, only to find that people oppose you yet again. This also happened to the Apostle Paul, for when he went to his beloved fellow Jews, they did not want to hear from him. Yet when he went to the Gentiles, God opened doors and he was able to plant a church. Yet even after his success, opposition would arise and that was Paul's eviction notice alerting him that it was time to move on to another field of work.

It's important to see in both instances of Isaac and Paul that God used opposition to direct their steps. He was sending them to a place where they were celebrated and not just tolerated, and when they got there, they both knew they were where they were supposed to be. God made room for them and He will do the same for you.

Are you ready to go where you are celebrated, or will you stubbornly stay and insist that where you are is where God must bless you? Do you see that it may not be a geographic relocation, but a shift to a different job, career, or people group that doesn't dread seeing you, but welcomes you gladly? Can you accept that even if you have failed, God will use that by taking you away from those who can only remember your failure to a people who don't know and don't care because you are God's answer to their prayers?

God wants you to know His will and the place where you will bear the most fruit. Therefore, don't fight His plan, but rather go with the flow, confident that God is making room for you by sending you into situations where you are celebrated for who you are and what you bring—and not resented for the same reasons.

5
Free To Be You

As we have seen, Abraham built more than a few altars during his pilgrimage to and from his land God had given him. Isaac built an altar too as we read in Genesis 26:23- 25:

> From there he went up to Beersheba. And the Lord appeared to him the same night and said, "I am the God of Abraham your father. Fear not, for I am with you and will bless you and multiply your off-spring for my servant Abraham's sake." So he built an altar there and called upon the name of the Lord and pitched his tent there. And there Isaac's servants dug a well (Genesis 26:23-25).

As one would expect, Isaac's son, Jacob, followed in his father's and grandfather's footsteps and built multiple altars, and also assigned names to a few areas important to him on his journey back home

1. Jacob also went on his way, and the angels of God met him. When Jacob saw them, he said, "This is the camp of God!" So he named that place Mahanaim (Genesis 32:1).

2. So that day Esau started on his way back to Seir. Jacob, however, went to Sukkoth, where he built a place for himself and made shelters for his livestock. That is why the place is called Sukkoth (Genesis 33:16-17) (note: he did *not* build an altar here).

3. After Jacob came from Paddan Aram, he arrived safely at the city of Shechem in Canaan and camped within sight of the city. For a hundred pieces of silver, he bought from the sons of Hamor, the father of Shechem, the plot of ground where he pitched his tent. There he set up an altar and called it El Elohe Israel (Genesis 33:18-20).

4. Then God went up from him at the place where he had talked with him. Jacob set up a stone pillar at the place where God had talked with him, and

he poured out a drink offering on it;
he also poured oil on it. Jacob called
the place where God had talked with
him Bethel (Genesis 35:13-15).

Please note that the Lord didn't tell Jacob
what to name the areas, which resembles the story of Adam naming the animals. This indicates
Jacob acted on those occasions out of his own
free will, using the creativity and ability to think
God gave him—just as Adam had done. It doesn't
seem God was displeased when either Isaac or
Jacob acted in that manner.

Yet there was one instance where God did
tell Jacob to go back and build: "Go up to Bethel
and settle there, and build an altar there to God,
who appeared to you when you were fleeing from
your brother Esau" (Genesis 35:1). God wanted Jacob to build an altar so he would be sure to
commemorate the encounter he had with God on
his way back home to see his brother after a sep-
aration of many years. Jacob obeyed, built an altar, and had another encounter with God that led
him to build the altar mentioned in number four
above.

What we see in these examples is Jacob
freely expressing his worship and creativity in
each instance, except for the one where God

clearly directed him. **What are the implications of this pattern for you?** It seems that you may have more freedom to express your purpose than you may have previously understood.

Are you waiting for God to direct your purpose and creativity, otherwise you refuse to do anything? Do you see that God can and will direct them, but not necessarily on every occasion? How will this impact your strategy and approach to your creative expressions and how you fulfill your purpose? Does this give you more freedom to be who God made you to be?

I have written dozens of books because I'm a writer. Writers write books so I don't have to pray about every project, but there are certainly times where it was clear the Lord instructed me to write—or help someone else write their book. You're God's partner, not His robot, and that fact should free you to express who you are without fear that somehow God is offended that you're stepping out and into who He made you to be.

6
Right In Front
Of Her Eyes

In this entry, let's look at the first of many instances recorded in the Bible when God opened someone's eyes to see what they could not otherwise see:

> Early the next morning Abraham took some food and a skin of water and gave them to Hagar. He set them on her shoulders and then sent her off with the boy. She went on her way and wandered in the Desert of Beersheba. When the water in the skin was gone, she put the boy under one of the bushes. Then she went off and sat down about a bowshot away, for she thought, "I cannot watch the boy die." And as she sat there, she began to sob. God heard the boy crying, and the angel of God called to Hagar from heaven and said to her,

"What is the matter, Hagar? Do not be afraid; God has heard the boy crying as he lies there. Lift the boy up and take him by the hand, for I will make him into a great nation." Then God opened her eyes and she saw a well of water. So she went and filled the skin with water and gave the boy a drink (Genesis 21:14-19).

Hagar found herself abandoned in the wilderness desert. We all know what a desert is like: hot in the day, cold at night, with no food or water. Hagar was convinced that once their water ran out, her son was doomed to die a slow death—as was she. It was in the midst of her grief that the Lord broke in and spoke to her, promising that her son would not die but would rather become a great nation. After God directed her to take the boy by the hand, God opened her eyes and there she saw a well of water. My question is: **Did that well suddenly and miraculously appear from heaven or was it there all along?**

My own sense is that the well was there all along but Hagar couldn't see it. Why couldn't she see it? She was blind to its existence because of her thinking. After all, they were in the desert where *everyone* knows there's no water, so that preconceived notion caused her not to see or even think to look for some. It's not that God had to heal her eyes, for there was nothing physically wrong with them. God had to change her thinking before she could see what was right in front of her all along.

What are the implications of this story for you? Where is your thinking preventing you from seeing your potential? Where have poverty thoughts caused you to be blinded to your riches in Christ? Where have ideas over your own limitations not allowed you to consider or pursue activities that are beyond what you think are your capabilities? Where have you even limited God because of your narrow or erroneous view of what He will and will not do?

The good news is that God wants to open your eyes. He did it for Hagar and she didn't even ask, so He will do it for you when you make the request, "Open my eyes, Lord, to see what I'm not seeing!" Pray that prayer today and then do like Hagar: Get up, take your purpose and creativity by the hand as Hagar did with Ishmael, give them a good drink of encouragement, and then get about the work of making your ideas what God sees they can be instead of what you have limited them to be.

7
Face The Truth

In John 4, we read the story of Jesus' trip home to Galilee that took Him through Samaria where He met an unnamed woman by a well. It's interesting that God ministered to Hagar by a well in the same region and I wonder whether the John 4 story took place at the same well. The Bible is silent on whether that's the case, but we do know that God did use wells to teach spiritual lessons to both women. And the women in both stories were victims of abusive behavior, being shunned by their cultures and peers, but were more than welcome to have a relationship with God.

Correct Doctrine

Jesus was at the well waiting for the disciples to come back with food when He shocked the women by asking her to give Him a drink of water: "'You are a Jew and I am a Samaritan woman. How can you ask me for a drink?' (For Jews do not associate with Samaritans.)" (John 4:9). When Jesus entered into a dialogue with the woman, however, she was more interested in discussing religion and doctrine concerning which mountain was the correct venue for worship than anything else.

This should sound familiar, for some in the Church today are still debating that topic (appropriate worship styles) and others are searching for correct dogma on other matters. When the woman asked for the living water Jesus mentioned, Jesus put her on the right path to establish a relationship with Him that would release the water she was seeking:

> Jesus answered, "Everyone who drinks this water will be thirsty again, but whoever drinks the water I give them will never thirst. Indeed, the water I give them will become in them a spring of water welling up to eternal life. The woman said to him, "Sir, give me this water so that I won't get thirsty and have to keep coming here to draw water." He told her, "Go, call your husband and come back" (John 4:13-16).

This woman didn't need correct doctrine; instead, she needed a correct perspective on her own spiritual condition. She was so used to thinking that if she believed right then she was right that she tricked herself into thinking her own spiritual condition and behavior were secondary to doctrine. Because Jesus loved her, He couldn't leave her in that state of deception.

Reality

The woman could have lied and said she had a husband who was busy or away on business. She could have gone home and had the man she was living with come back with her and pretend to be her husband. The beauty of her story is that she told Jesus the truth: She had no husband. It was then that Jesus revealed to her who He truly was and the woman went back to her village saying, "He told me everything I ever did" (John 4:39). Notice that her truth didn't disqualify her from a relationship with Jesus or revelation from Him, but was actually her starting point. Jesus told the woman not only to face the truth, but face it and then come back to Him.

The woman's reality was the place from which she was to worship. Jesus told her, "Yet a time is coming and has now come when the true worshipers will worship the Father in the Spirit and in truth, for they are the kind of worshipers the Father seeks. God is spirit, and his worshipers must worship in the Spirit and in truth" (John 4:23-24). Your truth in worship isn't only the truth of who Jesus is but the reality of who you are and are not—not who you're pretending to be, hope to be, or who you think others want you to be.

Jesus is saying to you what He said to the woman: Go, face the reality of who you are, and then approach me on that basis. That reality isn't only your deficiencies, but also your strengths, gifts, and insight He has given you. When will you realize that if you're good enough for God, you should be good enough for yourself? Stop trying to spit shine and polish an image of who you think you need to be and accept who you are. When the woman at the well did that, she found Jesus in a way that all those in Israel who were seeking (and thought they were finding) doctrinal truth couldn't find Him.

As you make the journey into self-awareness, you'll learn that it's your ticket and highway to spiritual growth. Face your reality—your fears and courage, strengths and weaknesses, gifts and purpose, boundaries and opportunities—and after you do, make sure you report back to Jesus no matter what you find. He already knows what's there, but wants you to know so you can work for Him with a foundation of truth that will always set you free to go, face even more truth, and then come back to Jesus again and again.

8
No Tools

Throughout Deuteronomy, we read the instructions Moses gave the people for what to do when they entered the Land as we read in this passage:

> "And when you have crossed the Jordan, set up these stones on Mount Ebal, as I command you today, and coat them with plaster. Build there an altar to the Lord your God, an altar of stones. Do not use any iron tool on them. Build the altar of the Lord your God with fieldstones and offer burnt offerings on it to the Lord your God. Sacrifice fellowship offerings there, eating them and rejoicing in the presence of the Lord your God. And you shall write very clearly all the words of this law on these stones you have set up" (Deuteronomy 25:4-8).

26

The people were to erect an altar of stones, but they were not to beautify or perfect it. Instead, they were to use the stones as they were, but they were to write the words of the law on them.

God was teaching the people that their worship and sacrifices at the altar weren't acceptable to Him through their effort, no matter how many sacrifices they made or how beautiful they could make their altar. Their worship was to be based on His words and the focus was to be on what God had done and was doing—not on their abilities or creativity. It was the words of the Law that sanctified the stones, not the work of the people. What's more, their sacrifices and worship weren't to be drudgery. They were to eat there, rejoicing in the presence of God.

The worship of God is a pretty simple matter of the heart, but we have often made it a flowery, ornate outward show of pomp and performance. You should strive in your walk with the Lord to get in touch with the concept Paul described in 2 Corinthians 11:3: "But I am afraid that just as Eve was deceived by the serpent's cunning, your minds may somehow be led astray from your *sincere and pure devotion to Christ*" (emphasis added).

How are your altars these days? Are they

places of joy or has legalism or boredom set into your life and work? Are you doing what gives you joy and worshiping God through it, or working to get a check? Are you worshiping God in spirit and truth—the truth of who you are and the beauty of who He is? What can you do to instill an element of wonder and exhilaration in the work of your hands?

9
A Prayer And A Plan

In this entry, let's look at how God used a well to answer Abraham's servant's prayer so you too can be encouraged in the tasks God has assigned you to do. In Genesis 24, we see that it was time for Isaac, Abraham's son of promise, to marry. For this to occur, Abraham had to exercise faith on his son's behalf:

> "I want you to swear by the Lord, the God of heaven and the God of earth, that you will not get a wife for my son from the daughters of the Canaanites, among whom I am living, but will go to my country and my own relatives and get a wife for my son Isaac" (Genesis 24:3-4).

Abraham commissioned his trusted servant to go to an unfamiliar land and find an unknown woman who would agree to come back with the servant to marry a man [Isaac] she had never met.

That could have been labeled mission impossible, but the story doesn't indicate the servant hesitated or complained. Instead, he saddled up and headed out to fulfill his master's command:

> Then the servant left, taking with him ten of his master's camels loaded with all kinds of good things from his master. He set out for Aram Naharaim and made his way to the town of Nahor. He had the camels kneel down near the well outside the town; it was toward evening, the time the women go out to draw water (Genesis 24:10-11).

What did he do when he got there? Did he put out the word and set up a series of interviews with potential candidates? Did he begin to ask around the area for references and leads? Did he put an ad in the local paper or post something on social media? (of course he didn't do that, but you get the idea). No, this faithful servant came up with a prayer and a plan:

> Then he prayed, "Lord, God of my master Abraham, make me successful today, and show kindness to my master Abraham. See, I am standing beside this spring, and the daughters of the

townspeople are coming out to draw water. May it be that when I say to a young woman, 'Please let down your jar that I may have a drink,' and she says, 'Drink, and I'll water your camels too'——let her be the one you have chosen for your servant Isaac. By this I will know that you have shown kindness to my master" (Genesis 24:12-14).

The servant had faith, came up with a faith plan, and then prayed and turned His plan over to God. What was the result? The first, yes the *first* woman who came to the well was the answer to his prayer:

Before he had finished praying, Rebekah came out with her jar on her shoulder. She was the daughter of Bethuel son of Milkah, who was the wife of Abraham's brother Nahor. The woman was very beautiful, a virgin; no man had ever slept with her. She went down to the spring, filled her jar and came up again (Genesis 24:15-16).

Have you refused certain tasks because you considered them impossible? Are you facing what you think are impossible tasks? Then think again and take a lesson from this servant's handbook. You should be creative like he was, come up with a plan, pray, and then watch God move on your behalf. After all, you too are a servant of the Most High God who has also given you an assignment to fulfill your purpose, but has not left you to do it alone. He is present to help you do what He has assigned, but you must have the faith and apply the creativity to help make the assignment come to a successful conclusion.

10
A Water Gift

Let's look at a story that indicates the love the people had for David:

> At that time David was in the stronghold, and the Philistine garrison was at Bethlehem. David longed for water and said, "Oh, that someone would get me a drink of water from the well near the gate of Bethlehem!" So the three mighty warriors broke through the Philistine lines, drew water from the well near the gate of Bethlehem and carried it back to David. But he refused to drink it; instead, he poured it out before the LORD. "Far be it from me, LORD, to do this!" he said. "Is it not the blood of men who went at the risk of their lives?" And David would not drink it (2 Samuel 23:15-17).

David uttered his wish to drink some of his favorite hometown water within earshot of some of his troops. Three of his men then took it upon themselves to risk their lives to fulfill David's wish. They broke through enemy lines, drew the water, and brought it back to David, fully expecting him to savor every drop. Instead, David refused to drink it and poured it out on the ground as a drink offering to the Lord! Imagine how those men must have felt when David did that. What was David thinking?

While David occasionally acted in his own self-interest with devastating results, for most of his reign (and even before it), he put the peoples' needs ahead of his own. He used his power to empower others and the list of his mighty men in 2 Samuel 23 proves that point. For David, leadership wasn't about him; it was about others.

The Lessons

David couldn't accept their gift of water because the people had risked their lives to get it. He knew that kind of commitment should be reserved for God and God alone. He had no intention of receiving it because there was the danger for him and for all leaders that they would think they deserved the sacrifice and effort because of who they are and how God wants to bless them. You would do well to have this same attitude as you serve in the position God has given you.

As you sit on your throne of purposeful living, it's not really about you. First, it's about God who put you there so you can serve His interests. Second, any leadership power and authority you have are to empower others and not build your own kingdom. Third, you are a first among equals with your followers and peers, and there's no room for arrogance or pride. You have what you have by the grace of God, not by your own efforts (although getting to where you are required a lot of effort).

David refused a gift that he saw as something of which only God was worthy. As you enjoy your time on the throne of your purpose where you rule and reign with Christ, you will do well to keep your and others' focus on God's interests, careful not to be confused as to why He put you where you are. If you do that, then you will thrive and not just survive as you carry out your unique, God-given assignment—and you will avoid using people as a means to get what it is that you want as opposed to what God wants.

11
Rivers Of Living Water

You are probably familiar with John 7:38:

> "Whoever believes in me, as the Scripture has said, streams of living water will flow from within him."

There's a flow that is to come out of you due to the Spirit's presence, and the "water" from that flow should taste like you. You can't allow it to become bitter with anger or unforgiveness, and it can't be salty with lies and deception. Also, it should not be artificially flavored to taste like someone else's water. In other words, the water should taste like you. Your flow should have your distinct characteristics—your personality, gifts, vocabulary, etc.—as you carry out God's work. This is just how God wants it to be so you should not apologize for or be self-conscious about this.

My writing, speaking, and consulting has my "flavor," and it flows. **How about you? Are you damming up the flow, trying not to be who** you are? Or are you filtering the water for im-purities and then letting it gush from your life? What's more, the water that flows isn't for your benefit; it's for others to drink. So in this case, it's alright for people to drink your flavored water.

Is there anything you enjoy doing or be-ing that you're trying to curtail or even adjust? Maybe it's part of your flow and you should stop interfering. Perhaps that characteristic is some-thing God built into you. When you oppose it, you're actually opposing God, telling Him He made a mistake when He put that in you.

In light of this truth, I'll continue to be who God made me to be, not worrying either about why I enjoy doing something as much as I do or what others are thinking. I just want to be who God made me to be and if anyone has a problem with that, it's their problem and not mine.

12
Excellence

When we begin to read Leviticus, we notice something right away in the first few verses:

> "If the offering is a burnt offering from the herd, you are to offer a male without defect" (Leviticus 1:3).

If you go on and read the first few chapters, you learn that this offering as well as all the others mentioned in the first few chapters were to be "without defect" or of the highest quality. Of course, all the offerings are a shadow of the One who was yet to come who was without defect—the sinless, morally perfect Son of Man. Yet, there could be another application to this truth. It indicates that whatever we do, we should produce a level of excellence in it because it is for the Lord and in His service.

I have been careful over the years to differentiate between perfection and excellence. The former is an elusive pursuit but excellence is within everyone's reach if this definition holds true: "excellence is doing all you do with a right heart and in a manner worthy of God." The right heart aspect means you're not doing what you do with any ulterior motives and the manner worthy of God speaks to the fact that God is deserving of your best efforts.

That means your work, play, creativity, and any other role or activity require the best of who you are and what you can do. William Temple, once the Archbishop of Canterbury, had this to say about excellence: "At the root of all your being, your intellectual studies, the games you play, whatever it is, the impulse to do them well is and ought to be understood as being an impulse towards God, the source of all that is excellent."

Do you pursue excellence in all you do, especially where your purpose and creativity are concerned? Do you attempt to give God your best? Do you see excellence as a spiritual matter and not just an academic or personal one? It's important you remember that excellence isn't perfection, it's doing your best and going above and beyond the minimum effort required. You do that because the God you serve is excellent and you are called to reflect Him in all you do.

13
The Burnt Offering

The Lord gave instructions for six specific offerings that the priests were to make on behalf of the people:

> ". . . the burnt offering, the grain offering, the sin offering, the guilt offering, the ordination offering and the fellowship offering" (Leviticus 7:38).

Instructions for the burnt offering were given first and it was the only offering that wasn't to be eaten by the priests. It was to be totally consumed by the fire on the altar:

> "Give Aaron and his sons this command: 'These are the regulations for the burnt offering: The burnt offering is to remain on the altar hearth throughout the night, till morning, and the fire must be kept burning on the altar'" (Leviticus 6:9).

Why wasn't the burnt offering to be consumed? It was the only offering that was for God and God alone. It was specifically to restore the people's fellowship and relationship with God because He was to be the first priority in the hearts and minds of the people. The same is true for believers today.

As you carry out your purpose and express your creativity, you will do what you do for the benefit of others. Yet your motivation for what you do must not be for the people. First and foremost, it must be for the Lord because it is His will and will please Him. That means when people ignore, disrespect, misuse, abuse, or take advantage of your good deeds, as they often do, you are to continue to do the good and purposeful things you have been assigned to do for the Lord and for Him only.

Remember, Jesus was sent to His own but they rejected Him, yet He continued and completed His mission because it was a burnt offering—He did it because it was the Father's will, which Jesus willingly chose to do. You follow in His footsteps when you pick up your cross and do the same.

So as you reflect further on the concept of the burnt offering, consider these questions. **Are you doing what you do for the Lord and not for others? Where have people problems caused** you to back off doing what only you can do? Are you angry or hurt over the lack of gratitude or recognition from those you work for or serve? Do you see that your fire must not go out and that you must do what you do for Him regardless of the response (or lack of it) from others?

From time to time, God will check your motives to see why you're doing what you do. That's so you won't derive your identity or sense of purpose from people or circumstances, both of which can be fickle. Instead, He will help you keep your focus on Him who is the ultimate rewarder of your efforts. When you serve the Lord, even if He is an audience of one, you are positioned properly to receive your eternal reward from the One who assigned your work in the first place.

14
Priestly Fire

The book of Leviticus is all about the priest—his duties and purpose in the nation's life. In fact, the priest is mentioned 143 times in Leviticus. Here is one of those mentions with a description of some of the priest's duties:

> The Lord said to Moses: "Give Aaron and his sons this command: 'These are the regulations for the burnt offering: The burnt offering is to remain on the altar hearth throughout the night, till morning, and the fire must be kept burning on the altar. The priest shall then put on his linen clothes, with linen undergarments next to his body, and shall remove the ashes of the burnt offering that the fire has consumed on the altar and place them beside the altar. Then he is to take off these clothes and put on others, and carry the ashes outside the camp to a place that is

ceremonially clean. The fire on the altar must be kept burning; it must not go out. Every morning the priest is to add firewood and arrange the burnt offering on the fire and burn the fat of the fellowship offerings on it. The fire must be kept burning on the altar continuously; it must not go out" (Leviticus 6:8-13).

Notice that the priest had to wear "linen undergarments" for he always had to carry out his job in a way that was dignified and formal. They all had the responsibility to ensure that the fire on the sacrificial altar never went out, for they were always on duty on behalf of the people as their mediator before God.

Now we are "a chosen people, a royal priesthood, a holy nation" (1 Peter 2:9) and have no need for the sacrificial fire. However, we do need the fire of the Holy Spirit and the best way to never allow that fire to go out is to keep doing what we love to do. In other words, you can keep the fire of God by flowing in your purpose and expressing your creativity, things you love to do that energize you. In a sense, you're like the burning bush in your purpose: you burn brightly but are never consumed. Paul put it this way to Timothy: "For this reason I remind you to fan into flame the gift of God, which is in you through the laying on of my hands" (2 Timothy 1:6).

As you reflect on your role as God's priest, consider the following questions. **Do you take your priestly duties seriously? Are you wearing your linen undergarments, carrying out your priestly, royal duties with dignity and grace? Has the fire gone out on your altar? Do you burn brightly, on duty at all times to be who God made you to be? What can you do to stoke the flames and keep them burning?**

Your service to God isn't a sprint but a long-distance, lifetime marathon. There's no retirement but instead God wants to preserve a "re-fire-ment" in your work for Him. The good news is that the fire of your purpose doesn't have to ever go out unless you want it to, and I'm not sure why you would stop doing what you love, that which keeps the fire going, in order to do nothing at all.

15
Sin Offering

Some of the priest's offerings he made at the altar were to restore fellowship, and a few were to honor God, but most were to deal with the sins of the people, both intentional and unintentional:

"If the whole Israelite community sins unintentionally and does what is forbidden in any of the Lord's commands, even though the community is unaware of the matter, when they realize their guilt and the sin they committed becomes known, the assembly must bring a young bull as a sin offering and present it before the tent of meeting ... When a leader sins unintentionally and does what is forbidden in any of the commands of the Lord his God, when he realizes his guilt and the sin he has committed becomes known, he must bring as his offering a male goat without defect ... If any member of the community sins unintentionally and does what is forbidden in any of the Lord's commands, when they realize their guilt and the sin they have committed becomes known, they must bring as their offering for the sin they committed a female goat without defect" (Leviticus 4:13-14; 22-23; 27-28).

The community, leaders, and people were to be conscious of sins they committed or could have committed, even when they were unaware of them and only later became aware. If you're like most people when you read this, you think of sins that were committed, labeled in theology as sins of commission. **But what about the sins of omission, those being the good things you could have done but did not do? Is sin only the "bad" things you do but not also the "good" things you don't do, whether intentional or not? Isn't that also missing the mark, which is the literal meaning of the word sin?**

When you don't learn the language, don't the people who know that language miss hearing what you have to say? What about the book you don't write? Aren't potential readers deprived of your testimony or insight? What happens when you don't take the missions

trip? Don't the people with whom you could build a relationship miss out on your gifts and love?

The point is that the sacrifices were instituted to sensitize the people to the concept of sin, but keep in mind that sin isn't just what you do; it's also what you don't do that you could do but refused or neglected to do. Determine to be all you can be and to do all you are capable of doing, and if you become aware that you have ceased doing either, then you need to repent and get back on track to lead a fruitful and productive life.

16
Firstfruits

As the Lord explained the procedure He required for each of the tabernacle offerings, He had this to say about the grain offering:

> "Every grain offering you bring to the LORD must be made without yeast, for you are not to burn any yeast or honey in a food offering presented to the LORD. You may bring them to the LORD as an offering of the firstfruits, but they are not to be offered on the altar as a pleasing aroma" (Leviticus 2:11-12).

The offering wasn't to include yeast or honey for those would be additives that would cause the grain to be bigger or sweeter than it naturally was. The grain offering was to be composed of only fine flour, symbolic of the nature of Christ who was refined through the things He suffered. But let's focus on another aspect of this offering, which was that it could be presented as firstfruits.

What would it represent and symbolize if someone brought a firstfruits grain offering?

When it's harvest time on a farm, it requires that all things go as they should in a small window of time for there to be a successful harvest. For example, farmers could work the first day and get an abundant harvest only to have bad weather come and ruin the rest of what was in the field. The farmer offering firstfruits took some of the initial harvest and chose to offer it to the Lord, in essence saying, "God, what I'm giving you is the first yield from the harvest. I give it to You first to give thanks but also to make a faith statement that it's the first among more harvest yet to come. I'm trusting You that I'll be able to successfully finish the harvest I have begun, and as a token of my faith, I'm giving away some of what I already have—fully expecting it to be replaced and then some."

Firstfruits is a faith statement that there's more to come and therefore you don't have to hold on to the first fruits of your labors. What's more, the firstfruits are optional and not required or commanded. You can willingly give them to God in faith that you'll finish the task and reap the full harvest—with God's help. You're declaring that God oversaw the firstfruits and will continue to watch over what belongs to you.

How can you apply the principle of first-fuits to your purpose and creativity? Perhaps you can give away the first output of a new creative expression you have? Maybe it's a special offering from the returns of a new venture in your company or ministry? However you express it, firstfruits is a way of saying, "Thank You, God, for what I have, but I'm expecting more to come through Your help."

17
A Memorial

Let's continue to look at the grain offering which we began in the last chapter as found in Leviticus 2:

> "He shall take out the memorial portion from the grain offering and burn it on the altar as a food offering, an aroma pleasing to the Lord. The rest of the grain offering belongs to Aaron and his sons; it is a most holy part of the food offerings presented to the Lord" (2:9-10).

The grain offering was cooked in a pan, the grain having been mixed with oil and salt. The concoction was then to be consumed by the priests, except for part of it which was burned on the altar as an "aroma pleasing to the Lord." There's a lot of symbolism here, but let's restrict our attention to what is referred to as the "memorial portion."

The memorial portion is like saying a blessing over your food when you give thanks for God's provision. It's taking a part of what you have and dedicating it to the Lord as a remembrance of your source, thinking back over your history of how God has always provided for you and yours. You recognize that what you have, not only for food, but for all of life, comes from His hand. This memorial portion also serves as a faith boost for today, for in essence you're saying, "God, You've provided before and here You are, doing it again. I trust You today for what I will need tomorrow because of what You did yesterday."

What can you do today to give a memorial offering to the Lord? Can you dedicate some time and use your gifts to help and serve others as an offering to Him? Perhaps you can give a testimony from your archive of blessings? Or maybe you can embark on some new adventure by remembering the past and dedicating your new pathway to His purpose? Whatever you do, make sure you don't just memorialize the past but use it as an inspiration for your future.

18
More To Come

One of the festivals the Jews were to observe was called the Feast of Weeks. The New Testament refers to this as the feast of Pentecost. We read in Leviticus,

"From the day after the Sabbath, the day you brought the sheaf of the wave offering, count off seven full weeks. Count off fifty days up to the day after the seventh Sabbath, and then present an offering of new grain to the LORD. From wherever you live, bring two loaves made of two-tenths of an ephah of the finest flour, baked with yeast, as a wave offering of firstfruits to the LORD. Present with this bread seven male lambs, each a year old and without defect, one young bull and two rams. They will be a burnt offering to the LORD, together with their grain offerings and drink offerings—a food offering, an aroma pleasing to the LORD" (Leviticus 23:15-18).

This was actually an act that offered the firstfruits from the wheat harvest which we looked at in Chapter 16, which thanked the Lord that the harvest had started and made a faith statement that conditions would be favorable to complete the ingathering. It was an "advance" gift to God in anticipation of better things to come.

In the New Testament, God chose to send the Holy Spirit on the day of Pentecost, which was also an advance on the harvest that was to come as the disciples went forth to fulfill the Great Commission. The outpouring was an advance gift that spoke of more gifts to come, for each person who received the Spirit also received the Spirit's gifts along with clarity of purpose. In some ways, the Acts of the Apostles could be named the Acts of Purpose for each person who received the Spirit (the Twelve, Barnabas, Dorcas, Luke, the Apostle Paul among others) also received a purpose assignment that, in conjunction with their gifts, yielded much fruit for God's Kingdom.

Have you seen the Spirit's deposit in you as a pledge of good things to come? What fruit are you producing that's in line with this gift from God? Are you anticipating more fruit as

you grow and mature, or have you become complacent and satisfied with your status quo? What return is God receiving from His investment in you?

Those who celebrated the Feast of Weeks had harvested fruit but came before the Lord with an offering because of their great expectations of more to come. May you also offer to God what you have in anticipation that you will be even more fruitful as you mature and grow in Him.

19
Seasoned With Salt

There's a tendency to skip over parts of the first five books of the Pentateuch because they are irrelevant and detached from modern culture and understanding. As you read through the early chapters of Leviticus, there are treasures to be gained regarding the five Goldmine Principles (purpose, creativity, goals, time management, and faith) but like most gold, we have to dig them out. Here is one such gold nugget:

> "Season all your grain offerings with salt. Do not leave the salt of the covenant of your God out of your grain offerings; add salt to all your offerings" (Leviticus 2:13).

Why were the people required to add salt to their offerings? Let's see if we can determine the reason and its relevance for us.

A covenant is an unbreakable agreement or treaty between two parties. God instituted various covenants throughout the Old Testament and then Jesus stated He came to establish another or a new covenant. It seems that salt was a part of establishing a covenant between the parties, which would symbolize that the agreements were to be preserved at all costs. There are certainly more symbolic meanings to the salt but that will suffice for our purposes.

Leviticus 2 discusses the grain offering which was composed of the finest flour, symbolic of Jesus' ministry through which He was sifted and found to be perfect or "fine" like flour. The grain first had to be grown through a farmer's effort, then converted to flour, and then offered. As you create and express your purpose, you're growing the grain, so to speak, so that you and your work can be sifted and converted into fine flour. You are to add salt to what you do as a reminder that your work isn't a hobby but rather an assignment from the Lord—just like He assigned work to Adam and Eve in Genesis 2. You've made a covenant with God, or shall I say He has made it with you, and you are to carry out your work as a matter of obedience and not convenience.

Is there salt present in what you do? Are you doing it for Him under His direction? Are you faithful to express your gifts, fulfill your

purpose, and create to your heart's content? If so, then there is indeed salt in your grain offering and it will be preserved in God's memory, which will be one of a faithful servant who carried out His will in season and out.

20
Something To Look Forward To

The Lord laid out a calendar of annual events Israel was to observe, which included Passover, Pentecost, the Feast of Tabernacles, and the Day of Atonement. And of course, offerings were to be made during all of them:

> The Lord said to Moses, "Speak to the Israelites and say to them: 'These are my appointed festivals, the appointed festivals of the LORD, which you are to proclaim as sacred assemblies'" (Leviticus 23:1-2).

The Jews were to plan their year not around work but rather around an awareness of God and His worship requirements. These celebrations or commemorations sometimes required travel to Jerusalem and necessitated that the people interrupt the rhythm of their lives to acknowledge the Lord's presence as the sustainer of their nation.

What's more, the Jews always had something they were looking forward to and planning. It created traditions they would celebrate as a family. There was an overall pattern of life but it was never to become drudgery or dull. As they experienced a variety of life experiences, it was to enhance not only their worship but their creativity and purpose as well, for a break from their normal routine would energize their lives and keep them from a complacent, surprise-free lifestyle.

As you consider the concept of planning future events and offerings to the Lord, reflect on these questions. **What about you? Is your life dull and a tad boring? Do you plan some things in your future to which you can look forward that involve seeing new things or at least things outside your daily routine? Do you celebrate special times with family and friends?**

Can you step away from where you live and work, and venture out into places for events that will stimulate and breathe life into your normal routine? Where is fear acting like gravity, holding you to a set pattern which you cannot break?

21
Rest

The issue of the Sabbath is mentioned several times in Leviticus, the one below included in a discussion of all the festivals Israel was to celebrate:

> "There are six days when you may work, but the seventh day is a day of sabbath rest, a day of sacred assembly. You are not to do any work; wherever you live, it is a sabbath to the Lord" (Leviticus 23:3).

A comprehensive study of the Sabbath is beyond the scope or purpose of this book. However, today's verse uses the phrase "sabbath rest," so let's simply examine it with the concept of rest in mind.

When you're doing work you love, for which you're gifted and called, there's usually no need to shut down due to exhaustion or over-work. Purpose work always gives back the energy expended to do it, which is a good indication of whether or not you are in your life's work. **Do you look forward to Friday and dread Monday when you have to return to your job? Do you look for ways to get out of your work instead of into it?** If the answer is yes to those questions, then perhaps you're in the wrong work.

Jesus made this statement, "The Sabbath was made for man, not man for the Sabbath" (Mark 2:27). He added, "Which is lawful on the Sabbath: to do good or to do evil, to save life or to kill?" (Mark 3:4). In other words, God didn't designate a day and then require that people serve the day. The day was set aside to serve their best interests brought about through rest, worship, and replenishment in preparation for the work yet to be done. That day was to be for the good of people, not to bind them to legalistic observances and restrictions.

Do you find yourself worn out, mentally and/or physically? Or does your work energize you? What changes can you make to ensure that it does? What do you need to stop doing? Don't be afraid to examine those questions and get good answers, for to find the work you love enables you to enjoy a sabbath rest every day. That's because you won't work because you *have* to, you will work because you *get* to. With the former attitude, you take a Sabbath because you're in desperate need of rest. With the latter, you enjoy a Sabbath to savor your work and thank God for a purposeful existence, trusting that the best is yet to come.

22
Futility

Leviticus can be a difficult book to read because it includes so many tedious details that eventually tempt us to skip those chapters to get to the "good parts" that are more interesting. Chapters 13 and 14 are long chapters devoted to what to do in the event of a skin disease or bodily discharge. For example, here's a portion of the instruction for someone with a skin disease:

> The Lord said to Moses, "These are the regulations for any diseased person at the time of their ceremonial cleansing, when they are brought to the priest: The priest is to go outside the camp and examine them. If they have been healed of their defiling skin disease ... The person to be cleansed must wash their clothes, shave off all their hair and bathe with water; then they will be ceremonially clean. After this they may come into the camp, but they must stay outside their

tent for seven days. On the seventh day they must shave off all their hair; they must shave their head, their beard, their eyebrows and the rest of their hair. They must wash their clothes and bathe themselves with water, and they will be clean" (Leviticus 14:1-3, 8-9).

Again, our purpose isn't to examine the meaning or symbolism in what is written but to discover lessons that can make us more purposeful and creative. In this case, we should be grateful that Christ set us free from having to pay attention to and being consumed by rules and regulations that could never satisfy God or be good enough for our freedom or cleansing. Peter summed it up succinctly when he wrote,

> ... knowing that you were ransomed from the *futile* ways inherited from your forefathers, not with perishable things such as silver or gold, but with the precious blood of Christ, like that of a lamb without blemish or spot (1 Peter 1:18-19, ESV, emphasis added).

We have been set free from a futile lifestyle and worship not so we can do as we please, but to invest our time in purposeful activities instead of religious ones.

In his second letter, Peter wrote, "For if these qualities are yours and are increasing, they keep you from being ineffective or unfruitful in the knowledge of our Lord Jesus Christ" (2 Peter 1:8). Simply stated, God expects you to be effective and fruitful in your freedom you've found in Him. **Are you productive and effective in your knowledge of Him? What fruit can you point to that proves you are productive? What can you do to bear even more fruit now that you are free to serve and express who you are?**

Paul gave us a simple directive of what we're to do now that we are free in Christ: "You, my brothers and sisters, were called to be free. But do not use your freedom to indulge the flesh; rather, serve one another humbly in love" (Galatians 5:13). Make sure you are focusing your purpose and creativity on how they can benefit the lives of others and not just your own.

23
The Living
And The Clean

In Leviticus 11, the Lord laid out the guidelines for clean and unclean food and what to do when touching a dead body:

> "If an animal that you are allowed to eat dies, anyone who touches its carcass will be unclean till evening. Anyone who eats some of its carcass must wash their clothes, and they will be unclean till evening. Anyone who picks up the carcass must wash their clothes, and they will be unclean till evening" (Leviticus 11:39-40).

The rationale behind these laws has been debated and written about for centuries, but for this book, we're looking for clues and guidelines to help us be more purposeful and creative. How does Leviticus 11 relate to our study? It would seem that the Lord wanted the people to be ever conscious and meticulous concerning the clean and unclean, the living and the dead. Is there any correlation to a New Testament principle?

Perhaps we could find that in what Jesus said in Mark 7:15: "Nothing outside a person can defile them by going into them. Rather, it is what comes out of a person that defiles them." We are to be as conscious and meticulous today concerning what is in us as the Jews were to their dietary laws. God wants clean and living things to come out of us, things that will edify others and glorify Him.

As you consider what I just wrote, reflect on these questions. **Are you around things that for you are clean and bring life? Are you then producing things that "come out of you" that are also clean and life-giving? Do you see now why it is so important to attend to your words and actions, for as James wrote, "Neither can a salt spring produce fresh water" (James 3:12)?**

You must keep your springs fresh and good tasting so you can produce the same in accordance with the gifts and purpose God has assigned you. Therefore, don't devote yourself to things that are below your high calling as a creator and servant of the Most High.

24
Staying Sober

When Aaron and his sons were on duty in the tent of meeting where they performed their priestly rituals, this is what the Lord required:

> "You and your sons are not to drink wine or other fermented drink whenever you go into the tent of meeting, or you will die. This is a lasting ordinance for the generations to come, so that you can distinguish between the holy and the common, between the unclean and the clean, and so you can teach the Israelites all the decrees the Lord has given them through Moses" (Leviticus 10:8-11).

This stipulation is similar to someone who voluntarily entered into what was called a Nazirite vow. A Nazirite wasn't to cut their hair, drink wine, or partake of any grape products whatsoever. Why no wine? It was perhaps because of wine's possible uses and side effects:

1. Wine deadens one's senses or pain, and Aaron and his sons were to be fully aware when they were handling or representing God and His business, even in the difficult things of life.

2. Wine could also be used during festive celebrations to enhance one's mood of joy. The Nazirites only source of joy was to be their total dedication to God's purpose in their lives.

We could spend more time on wine and what it represents, but in the context of this story, it would seem that Aaron wasn't permitted to do anything that would help him cope with or enhance his life except to do the work and be the representative God had chosen him to be (see the next chapter).

Perhaps it could be likened today to the many ways people try to escape or deal with their pain and responsibilities. They do so through things like binge watching TV, shopping, eating, family drama, or other activities that in and of themselves are not evil or wrong until they are used as a means to avoid the realities of one's human experience and current situation.

Read what Peter wrote, keeping in mind that his exhortation to "sobriety" wasn't a warning against the consumption of alcohol but a directive that you're to keep your wits and spiritual perspective about you at all times:

> Be alert and of sober mind. Your enemy the devil prowls around like a roaring lion looking for someone to devour. Resist him, standing firm in the faith, because you know that the family of believers throughout the world is undergoing the same kind of sufferings (1 Peter 5:8-10).

God is to be the source of your help in times of trouble and temptation. **Are you pressing into Him during difficult times? Are you embracing your call or frittering away your time on empty diversions? Is your creativity all it can be or do you keep yourself occupied with lesser things to keep yourself from disappointment or failure?**

Those who now work for God in His kingdom aren't to waste or divert their energy away from Kingdom activity. They are to stay awake and alert (sober) at all times and in all things.

25
Focused

There's an account in Leviticus 10 that makes the Old Testament for some so scary and foreboding, and it ties into the issue we discussed in the previous chapter:

> Aaron's sons Nadab and Abihu took their censers, put fire in them and added incense; and they offered unauthorized fire before the Lord, contrary to his command. So fire came out from the presence of the Lord and consumed them, and they died before the Lord (Leviticus 10:1-2).

One denomination uses these verses as a warning that we are not to use musical instruments in worship for they aren't mentioned in the New Testament and are thus the equivalent of offering "strange fire" before the Lord. Others look at this event as an example of God's holiness that isn't to be trifled with in any way, shape, or form.

Let's skip over trying to figure out exactly why this happened and look at the instructions that followed:

> Then Moses said to Aaron and his sons Eleazar and Ithamar, "Do not let your hair become unkempt and do not tear your clothes, or you will die and the Lord will be angry with the whole community. But your relatives, all the Israelites, may mourn for those the Lord has destroyed by fire. Do not leave the entrance to the tent of meeting or you will die, because the Lord's anointing oil is on you" (Leviticus 10:6-11).

Aaron, the dead men's father, wasn't permitted to mourn as the other relatives. He was to keep his focus as a leader and priest because "the Lord's anointing oil" was upon him and his sons. The same is true for you. This isn't to insinuate that you can't have family relationships or feel what they feel. It doesn't mean you can't mourn the loss of a loved one.

However, even Jesus was quite clear that nothing, not even family, was to interfere or, perhaps better to say, to be a higher priority than God's purpose in your life: "Anyone who loves their father or mother more than me is not worthy of me; anyone who loves their son or daughter more than me is not worthy of me. Whoever does not take up their cross and follow me is not worthy of me" (Matthew 10:37-39). You have work to do and God will help you do it if you stay diligent and disciplined.

On what part of your life is God's anointing oil most evident? Are you focused on your purpose and creativity, or do you put them off until in your mind all the conditions of your life are conducive to doing them? Where do you need to be more focused and structured?

Don't take God's anointing for granted or make light of its importance in your life and in God's plan for you.

26
Guidance

When Leviticus completed the instructions for the sacrifices in chapter 7, it moved on to the ordination of the priesthood. First, it described the garments the priests were to wear, including this obscure reference to something called the Urim and Thummim:

> "He placed the breastpiece on him and put the Urim and Thummim in the breastpiece" (Leviticus 8:8).

What exactly were the Urim and Thummim? We aren't quite sure but it seems they were precious stones embedded in the portion of the priest's garment that was over his heart. These stones served as a source of guidance for the nation at critical junctures in their history.

How did they operate? Again, we aren't sure, but conjecture is that they glowed or somehow reflected light or energy that would indicate God's will when they were consulted. There are less than a dozen references to the Urim and Thummim in the Old Testament and we don't have a record of how often they were consulted or why they seemed to disappear from existence and use. We just know they existed.

One thought is that God directed the people to go to their spiritual leaders for advice because they didn't have any Scriptures to consult. They didn't have a copy of the Law or a Bible they could search for answers. They were learning how to follow the Lord and trust the fact that He communicated to His people through His designated leaders.

As Israel grew and matured, perhaps there was less need for them to consult the Urrim and Thummim, which is the reason for the lack of references to them. The main takeaway from their existence, however, is that God was ready to guide His people whenever they asked Him to do so. He led them by a cloud and pillar of fire as to where they should go and how long they should stay. He gave His Law to instruct and inform their lives as to His worship requirements. Then He provided these stones in the priests' garments for specific requests.

If that is what God was willing to do "back then," what is He capable of doing today through His Word, His spiritual leaders, and the guidance of the Holy Spirit that dwells

in each believer? What's more, do you trust Him to lead you or are you afraid that somehow even when you ask, the answer might get garbled in transmission? Or that God will trick or entice you to do something you aren't supposed to do?

When it comes to God's guidance, keep in mind what James wrote:

> If any of you lacks wisdom, you should ask God, who gives generously to all without finding fault, and it will be given to you. But when you ask, you must believe and not doubt, because the one who doubts is like a wave of the sea, blown and tossed by the wind. That person should not expect to receive anything from the Lord. Such a person is double-minded and unstable in all they do (James 1:5-8).

You can be confident that God will answer your cries for guidance with specific feedback that will enable and empower you to do His will on every occasion. **Are you asking? Are you trusting in His response? Are you acting on what you hear?**

27
Tailor–Made

We've seen that Leviticus established the guidelines for a variety of offerings, one of which was the peace or fellowship offering. This was a freewill offering in that it wasn't prescribed as a sacrifice for sin, but as an expression of thanksgiving or an act upon the fulfillment of a voluntary vow at the giver's discretion:

> These are the regulations for the fellowship offering anyone may present to the Lord: ... "If they offer it as an expression of thankfulness, then along with this thank offering they are to offer thick loaves made without yeast and with olive oil mixed in, thin loaves made without yeast and brushed with oil, and thick loaves of the finest flour well-kneaded and with oil mixed in. Along with their fellowship offering of thanksgiving they are to present an offering with thick loaves of bread made with yeast.

They are to bring one of each kind as an offering, a contribution to the Lord; it belongs to the priest who splashes the blood of the fellowship offering against the altar. The meat of their fellowship offering of thanksgiving must be eaten on the day it is offered; they must leave none of it till morning" (Leviticus 7:1, 12-15).

Be honest. In all probability, you skip over reading passages like this and perhaps skip over the book of Leviticus altogether. Why? Because it gives too many details that seem irrelevant for life today. Yet Moses wrote this with great care because it was consistent with who he was. Moses wasn't a man given to inspiration from what we know of him. He was more in tune with the details. God gave him Ten Commandments and he spent the rest of His life explaining the implications of those commandments to the people, which produced the first five books of the Bible.

The point is that God will give you tasks tailor-made for who He created you to be, just like He did for Moses and others. Peter could inspire large crowds, Nehemiah organized large tasks, David composed moving poetry, and Lydia in Acts built a successful multi-national business.

What can you do better than most people? Are you fighting who you are, trying to be someone else? Do you accept that you can't do or be it all, instead trying to be the best you that you can be? What changes do you need to make that will position you to do work best suited to who He made you to be, just like Moses as he wrote his often tedious-to-read worship manual in Leviticus?

What's more, God has confidence you are up to completing the tasks He gives you because He made you and knows you better than you know yourself. Don't argue or debate with Him when He introduces an assignment. Instead think, *God, You know what You're doing so I accept this command, trusting that You will go with me as I obey.*

28
A Wave Offering

Let's look at another aspect of the fellowship offering, which we looked at in the previous chapter:

> The Lord said to Moses, "Say to the Israelites: 'Anyone who brings a fellowship offering to the Lord is to bring part of it as their sacrifice to the Lord. With their own hands they are to present the food offering to the Lord; they are to bring the fat, together with the breast, and wave the breast before the Lord as a wave offering'" (Leviticus 7:28-30).

The worshiper was to "wave the breast before the Lord as a wave offering." What happens when you wave to someone? You're drawing their attention to you, in essence saying, "Hello, I'm here. I send you greetings. I acknowledge your presence is within eyesight of my presence and I welcome it. Please respond and welcome me."

The wave offering was designed to say, "God, I see You and I hope You see me. Here I am, thanking You for your goodness and mercy. I hope you acknowledge my presence!" Then the rest of the offering was to be shared with others to eat and enjoy.

This offering counters the oft-heard exhortation that it must be all about the Lord while you do nothing to draw attention to yourself. The fellowship offering does the opposite. It's an expression of who you are, given when you choose to do so, and is for no other reason than to say to God, "Hi! I'm here and I know You are, too." That means you can wave your gift of poetry, business, teaching, mercy, missions, generosity, humor, or any other talent before the Lord and draw His attention to what you're doing as a means of worship and thanksgiving that He made you who you are. Then you can share who you are and what you do with others as another means of giving thanks.

What do you have that you can wave before the Lord? What do you have or do that you can share with others as part of your wave offering? What do you do that when the focus centers on you, you can then redirect the attention on Him, the One who gave you the gift or talent in the first place?

The point is that God doesn't have to initiate everything you do so you can use your free will and decide to give to God and others out of the abundance of who you are to show gratitude for who God made you to be.

29
A Drink Offering

But even if I am being poured out *like a drink offering* on the sacrifice and service coming from your faith, I am glad and rejoice with all of you. So you too should be glad and rejoice with me (Philippians 2:17-18 emphasis added).

What was a drink offering? It was a liquid offering that was poured over the body of a sacrificial animal or into the fire that consumed the animal. Regardless of how a drink offering was poured out, there was nothing left of it after it was poured. The ground either soaked it up and it disappeared, or it created a hissing sound as it evaporated due to the heat of the sacrificial fire.

Paul hoped to have something to boast about on the day of Christ as stated earlier in Philippians, but he was also content to have his labor consumed on the sacrifice and service of others' faith. He knew that if that happened, then only God would know what Paul had done. If Paul was a drink offering, relegated to obscurity and insignificance, he would be happy and rejoice in that, for Paul knew that God Himself would notice and reward him.

In verse 18, Paul asked the Philippians to join him in his joy if indeed his labor was somehow obscured or rendered seemingly useless and of no effect. Keep in mind that Paul was already an example of a drink offering, for he was writing this letter from prison. God's most effective apostle was on the bench, so to speak, not in the game but relegated to writing from his prison home.

Despite that, he was able to turn his work over to God, trusting Him for the results and the credit that would be given to him as a worker in God's kingdom. Later we read that this process had been completed: "For I am already being poured out like a drink offering, and the time for my departure is near" (2 Timothy 4:6).

How do you think you would feel if your life's work seemed to be rendered useless? What if you were a starter on the team but were then relegated to the bench? Could you rejoice? Would you rejoice?

Paul's trust in the Lord was so complete that he could entrust his results and legacy to the God who had called and empowered him. Keep his example in mind if at any time you or your work are dishonored and ignored by others, confident that they are written in God's book and are uppermost in His mind where you are concerned.

30
A River Altar

The Red Sea was not the only body of water the people had to cross to get to the Promised Land. Eventually they also had to cross the Jordan River. When they did so, Joshua gave them these instructions:

> When the whole nation had finished crossing the Jordan, the Lord said to Joshua, "Choose twelve men from among the people, one from each tribe, and tell them to take up twelve stones from the middle of the Jordan, from right where the priests are standing, and carry them over with you and put them down at the place where you stay tonight."

> So Joshua called together the twelve men he had appointed from the Israelites, one from each tribe, and said to them, "Go over before the ark of the LORD your God into the middle of

the Jordan. Each of you is to take up a stone on his shoulder, according to the number of the tribes of the Israelites, to serve as a sign among you. In the future, when your children ask you, 'What do these stones mean?' tell them that the flow of the Jordan was cut off before the ark of the covenant of the LORD. When it crossed the Jordan, the waters of the Jordan were cut off. These stones are to be a memorial to the people of Israel forever" (Joshua 4:1-7).

The Lord stopped the river flow so the people could cross as the priests stood in the river holding the ark of the covenant. The people were to commemorate the event by taking a stone out of the riverbed, one for each tribe to serve as a memorial.

You are also to "extract" things from the events of your life to help you remember God's goodness. You can do this through journaling to keep a written record. Perhaps you can establish a scholarship fund to be given every year in honor of God's goodness in your life, or make some other special offering to commemorate your memory. **What other things can you think of to build a memorial to God's faithfulness in your life?**

If your heart is to thank God and establish a way for your children and grandchildren to remember God's activity in their family's history, then God will give you a creative way to do just that.

31
A Tall Altar

In Genesis 10, we read about a people that spread out to fill the earth as the Lord had commanded them to do. In Genesis 11, we read about those who stopped spreading out and instead decided to stay put and build a tower, which in my mind was an oversized altar that was built to offer self-serving sacrifices instead of one's that glorified God:

> Now the whole world had one language and a common speech. As people moved eastward, they found a plain in Shinar and settled there. They said to each other, "Come, let's make bricks and bake them thoroughly." They used brick instead of stone, and tar for mortar. Then they said, "Come, let us build ourselves a city, with a tower that reaches to the heavens, so that we may make a name for ourselves; otherwise we will be scattered over the face of the whole earth" (Genesis 11:1-4).

These people wanted to make "a name for themselves," and they determined to do it at any cost. What did they do? They made bricks. They lived in a hot, desert climate, but decided to bake the bricks thoroughly, which meant they had to build fires, making an already unpleasant work environment even worse. Then they decided to use tar to hold the bricks together. Do you know what tar smells like when it's heated? If you do, you know it gives off a foul odor.

Contrast these conditions with those in the Garden and you will see what the Fall cost people in regards to their purpose and creativity and how they would ultimately be expressed. What's more, rather than spread *out* as they were command-ed, these people decided to *stay put* in one place and build *up*, believing they could reach heaven through their own effort and work.

Proverbs 13:15 states, "Good understand-ing giveth favour: but the way of transgressors is hard" (KJV) while Psalm 127:1-2 warns the reader, "Unless the Lord builds the house, the builders la-bor in vain. Unless the Lord watches over the city, the guards stand watch in vain. In vain you rise early and stay up late, toiling for food to eat—for he grants sleep to those he loves."

How would you characterize your work

and career? Do you enjoy your work or are you toiling away in the heat of the day in unpleasant conditions? Are you building a name for yourself or glorifying God? Have you stubbornly planted yourself in one place, perhaps enduring mistreatment and a harsh environment rather than move on to something else, like as if you have the only job on the planet? If you are making bricks in the desert, can you trust the Lord for something better? How will you find it?

God wants you to enjoy your work, which was the conclusion of the wisdom writer in Ecclesiastes 2:24-25: "A person can do nothing better than to eat and drink and find satisfaction in their own toil. This too, I see, is from the hand of God, for without him, who can eat or find enjoyment?" This fits in with what Paul wrote in Romans 12:1-2:

> Therefore, I urge you, brothers and sisters, in view of God's mercy, to offer your bodies as a living sacrifice, holy and pleasing to God—this is your true and proper worship. Do not conform to the pattern of this world, but be transformed by the renewing of your mind. Then you will be able to test and

approve what God's will is—his good, pleasing and perfect will.

Your reasonable act of worship that Paul mentioned is joyful activity offered to God through your altar of worship, which is a life yielded completely and totally to His purpose and will for you.

32
The Fear Factor

I wrote a book titled *Go and Obey: God's Call to Action* that emphasized God's bias for action, but this final thought will focus on mankind's resistance to that call to step out and do whatever it is God has spoken. While the refusal to go is based in people's rebellion against God and His authority, its roots are in fear, and that is why I have titled this entry, "The Fear Factor." Let's look at that concept now.

The Refusals

I can think of two cases where people refused when God told them to go. The first was Jonah, the reluctant prophet, who was told to go to Nineveh and deliver a hard word that God's judgment was coming. Instead of heading to Nineveh, Jonah got on a ship and went in the opposite direction. He eventually revealed that he didn't want to go because he knew the Lord would relent of His verdict if the people repented—which they did and He did. Jonah ended up going, but it was through the whale express that transported him to a spot within walking distance of his assigned destination.

The second refusal was on the part of the apostles, who had heard Jesus' words to go. The apostles, a title which means 'sent forth one,' chose to stay in their Jerusalem comfort zone. It took persecution for them to get up and go. They prove it is no guarantee that we will go just because we have heard from the Lord, something that many people claim to be true: "If only God would speak to me, *then* I would know and do His will."

On the one hand, Jonah was afraid God would change His mind, because Jonah wanted the inhabitants of Nineveh, the enemies of his people, to be wiped out. On the other hand the apostles were afraid of what their fellow Jews would say when they went to the Gentiles, so they didn't go, even with their marching orders in hand. The most significant refusal, however, is found in the Old Testament and we can learn more lessons from it by revisiting the Tower of Babel which we also looked at in Study 31.

A Tower And A City

The Lord told Adam and Eve, and then Noah, to be fruitful and fill the earth. God wanted

WELLS, ALTARS, AND OFFERINGS

them to go and spread out, but their descendants rebelled and stayed put. In Genesis 11, we read that the people decided to make a name for themselves, so they settled down to build a monument or tower to give themselves an identity and place they could call their own. What did the Lord do when they refused to go?

First, he confused their language and then,

> "The Lord scattered them from there over all the earth, and they stopped building the city. That is why it was called Babel—because there the Lord confused the language of the whole world. From there the Lord scattered them over the face of the whole earth" (Genesis 11:8-9).

This refusal to go was revisited and reversed at Pentecost in Acts 2 when God once again intervened, this time to give mankind a language of the Spirit that would restore their ability to obey God and go. As they went, the Spirit would this time aid their communication as evidenced by every man present in Acts 2 hearing God being extolled in their native tongue. Whereas before, God had confused their language, this time He would clarify it, so they could overcome a major barrier to going and that was the inability to communicate.

The people who built the tower were afraid. They were afraid to go out for whatever reason. Perhaps they were afraid they would lose their identity. Maybe they were fearful of what they would find as they went. They were willing to make bricks in the desert, adding heat to an already unbearable climate, just so they would not have to go.

Are you doing the same thing? Are you making bricks in the desert with people you don't understand (and who don't understand you)? Has God confused the communication between you and others because you are in the wrong place? Is all this rooted in the fear factor that if you go, you will somehow lose something instead of gaining?

When I say go, it doesn't mean you have to go far away (although you may). It does mean you must be in motion to take the initiative on what God has put in your heart to do. **Where is the fear factor keeping you from going and doing?**

As we close this series, I advise you to consider where you are and where God wants you to be. If they are not the same, then your work and way are probably hard. If you go, whether it's to go and write, go and speak, go and learn, go and build, go and proclaim, or go and create, then God will go with you and you will experience the true power of Pentecost. God will help you and it will be exhilarating. Your message will be clear because you are clear.

May the Lord reveal to you what your go is and then may you face and overcome your fear and obey, knowing that He will be with you to the ends of the earth—or to the end of your street, wherever it is He has chosen for you to serve. Have a blessed week!

Two Bonus Entries On The Theme Of Building

Since altars need to be built and wells to be dug, I thought it would be helpful to include two entries that specifically address the matter of building and doing it wisely as Jesus advised us to do. These entries are taken from my commentary series, Live the Word, so they are a different format than what you encountered so far in this book.

33
Sand Or Rock?

Let's look at the last words of Jesus' Sermon on the Mount in Matthew 7 where He concluded His message with some shocking words:

> "Not everyone who says to me, 'Lord, Lord,' will enter the kingdom of heaven, but only the one who does the will of my Father who is in heaven. Many will say to me on that day, 'Lord, Lord, did we not prophesy in your name and in your name drive out demons and in your name perform many miracles?' Then I will tell them plainly, 'I never knew you. Away from me, you evildoers!'" (Matthew 7:21-23).

Talk is cheap, even in church settings, where there are many who pay lip service to the Lord. There are times when I have done it myself, saying to God, "I surrender all, Lord," then refusing to surrender all. It sounded so spiritual and it was easy to say or sing, but it was only an emotional declaration, without any substance.

Jesus spoke to this human tendency, which can be deceptive to the extent that some believe they will enter God's kingdom through talk. The kingdom of God is God's government and only those who actually submit to God's government in their lives will enter and enjoy that Kingdom. The Kingdom doesn't belong to those who talk about the Lordship of God, but it does belong to those who submit to and carry out the will of the Lord.

To which day is Jesus referring in verse 22? He is referring to a day when we will appear before the Lord to evaluate the quality of our relationship with Him. Jesus indicated that some would have exercised spiritual gifts, but those gifts would not be an indicator of their obedience; they would have been evidence of God's love for His people. When I read this, I always think of the story of Saul and David:

> The next day an evil spirit from God came forcefully upon Saul. He was prophesying in his house, while David was playing the harp, as he usually did. Saul had a spear in his hand and he hurled it, saying to himself, "I'll pin David to the wall." But David eluded him twice (1 Samuel 18:10-11).

While Saul was prophesying, he tried to kill David. That proves spiritual gifts are *not* always an indicator of spirituality, maturity, or obedience.

Yet how could God say He didn't know these "evildoers"? I heard it explained that it would be like a human judge in a court of law who had to sentence one of their children. When that judge sat in the judgment seat, they would not "know" their child as such, but rather as someone who stood before them to be judged by the law that the judge had sworn to uphold. That judge could say, "I don't know you as my child. I must be impartial and judge you according to your actions, not according to our relationship."

Of course, any secular judge would recuse themselves from such a scenario so that they would not be accused of preferential treatment toward their child. God has no such problem, for He is an impartial and perfect judge. Consequently, He could say to one of His creatures, "I never knew you" as He judged their behavior and spoke the truth.

I don't know about you, but I want Him to know me in the best sense of the word now and when I stand before Him. For that to happen, I don't need to talk a good game, I need to live and play a good game that includes obedient action when God reveals His will for me. I need to build on the solid foundation of His word and not on the shifting sand of cultural trends or emotional needs.

34
Wise Builders

"Therefore everyone who hears these words of mine and puts them into practice is like a wise man who built his house on the rock. The rain came down, the streams rose, and the winds blew and beat against that house; yet it did not fall, because it had its foundation on the rock. But everyone who hears these words of mine and does not put them into practice is like a foolish man who built his house on sand. The rain came down, the streams rose, and the winds blew and beat against that house, and it fell with a great crash."

When Jesus had finished saying these things, the crowds were amazed at his teaching, because he taught as one who had authority, and not as their teachers of the law (Matthew 7:24-29).

I'm old enough now to have a better perspective on some life matters, and I've seen the long-term effects of people who built wisely and foolishly. The wise took Jesus' words and applied them with a view toward long-term success. Others looked for a shortcut and for a time seemed like they had found one. Yet when the pressures of life or when God tested their work, their life and work were found to be shabby and shaky.

You can't escape the fact that your work will be tested in this life. Jesus didn't say "*if* the winds blow" but rather "*when* the winds blow." Paul alluded to the same inevitability when he wrote:

> By the grace God has given me, I laid a foundation as an expert builder, and someone else is building on it. But each one should be careful how he builds. For no one can lay any foundation other than the one already laid, which is Jesus Christ. If any man builds on this foundation using gold, silver, costly stones, wood, hay or straw, his work will be shown for what it is, because the Day will bring it to light. It will be revealed with fire, and the fire will test the quality of each man's work. If what he has built survives, he will receive his

reward. If it is burned up, he will suffer loss; he himself will be saved, but only as one escaping through the flames (1 Corinthians 3:10-15).

I'm especially concerned with how many seem to offer financial shortcuts to God's people. Some promise great returns for a "seed gift" of a certain amount of money. I have heard some promise the gift of wisdom if someone donates $951, since there are 951 verses in the book of Proverbs. This is pure nonsense and is the equivalent of a spiritual lottery. People invest money in the hopes of "winning" a lot more wisdom. This is what takes place in a casino and should not take place around God's business. It's true that you give and God will bless you, but there's only one way to gain wealth: "In all labor there is profit, but mere talk leads only to poverty" (Proverbs 14:23).

You gain wealth by hard work, wise investments, and the grace of God. Those who come with promises of wealth if you give a gift to their work and ministry are frauds: "For we are not like many, peddling the word of God, but as from sincerity, but as from God, we speak in Christ in the sight of God" (2 Corinthians 2:17).

What is a peddler? The dictionary defines a peddler as "one who deals in or promotes something intangible (as a personal asset or an idea)." Don't look for spiritual shortcuts, for there aren't any. Build wisely, like a master builder, and put your hope and expectations in God for the long-term. **Have you been guilty of looking for and experimenting with shortcuts, especially where money or spiritual blessings are concerned?** If so, you need to repent and change your ways.

How To
Follow The Author

There you have my collections of essays and devotionals around the theme *Altars, Wells, and Offerings: Digging Deeper, Building Better, Offering More*. These are all taken from my various online publications, many of which are also now available in book form (both paper and e-book). If you would like to access more of these resources for your study or devotional reading, here is how to do so.

The Monday Memo

Every Sunday since 2001 I have written a Monday Memo to discuss topics like purpose, creativity, and faith. You can access it at: http://www.stankomondaymemo.com

The Stanko Bible Study

I have completed a verse-by-verse commentary on the New Testament and I am not writing a weekly entry in the Purpose Study Bible that examines the topics of purpose, creativity, goal setting, time management, and faith as they are found in the Old Testament. All these studies for both the Old and New Testaments can be found at http://www.stankobiblestudy.com.

All My Books

Are available for purchase on Amazon or through: http://www.urbanpress.us

My Free Mobile App

You can download the PurposeQuest app from https://subsplash.com/purposequestinternationa/app I have many hours of video and audio teaching there.

Your Daily Bible QUESTion

I produce a daily two-minute devotional called Your Daily Bible QUESTion, which can be found on all my social media outlets as well as on my mobile app. It also includes Spanish subtitles.

My Website

http://www.purposequest.com has all my video and audio teachings, plus some print material, but doesn't have the daily devotional.

Social Media

I publish daily material on all my social media outlets: Facebook, Instagram, Twitter, LinkedIn, TikTok, and YouTube. You can easily find and follow me on any of those outlets by using my first and last name.

And of course, I am always available through my email address: johnstanko@gmail.com

Made in the USA
Columbia, SC
06 November 2023

25145570R00070